The Gift of Confirmation Sponsors

For Sponsors of Children Being Confirmed

Mary Kathleen Glavich, SND

ACTA
ASSISTING CHRISTIANS TO ACT
PUBLICATIONS

The Gift of Confirmation Sponsors
For Sponsors of Children Being Confirmed
by Mary Kathleen Glavich, SND

Edited by Gregory F. Augustine Pierce
Cover design by Tom A. Wright
Typesetting by Desktop Edit Shop, Inc.
Cover art "Spirit Among Us" cast by Ars Liturgica Kunsterverlag Maria Laach,
        available from www.CreatorMundi.com. Used with permission.

Scripture excerpts are taken from the *New American Bible with Revised New Testament and Psalms,* copyright © 1991, 1986, 1970 by the Confraternity of Christian Doctrine, Inc., Washington, D.C. Used with permission. All rights reserved. No part of the *New American Bible* may be reproduced by any means without permission in writing from the copyright owner.

Copyright © 2004 by Mary Kathleen Glavich, SND

Published by: ACTA Publications
                 Assisting Christians To Act
                 4848 N. Clark Street
                 Chicago, IL 60640-4711
                 773-271-1030
                 www.actapublications.com

Library of Congress Card Number: 2003115219

ISBN: 0-87946-264-7

Printed in the United States of America

Year: 10 09 08 07 06 05 04
Printing: 10 9 8 7 6 5 4 3 2 1

Contents

Celebrating the Holy Spirit

Dear Sponsor,

Congratulations on being invited to be a confirmation sponsor. Being chosen for this special task is an honor, but you'll find that serving as a sponsor is a responsibility as well as a privilege.

You might feel that you are not "good" enough to be a sponsor. Apparently some people thought you were, and you should accept their judgment graciously. If you are a bit hesitant about being a sponsor and wonder what it entails, however, this book is for you. Reading the explanations about the sacrament of confirmation and getting ideas on what you might do with the child who is being confirmed will build your confidence and help you relate to the candidate entrusted to your care.

Through his or her baptism, the child you are sponsoring was first *initiated* into the Church, becoming a member of God's family and an heir to heaven. The Trinity—God the Father, God the Son, and God the Holy Spirit—came to dwell within him or her.

Baptism, however, is only the first of what the Church calls the three "sacraments of initiation": baptism, confirmation and Eucharist. The child is now being prepared intensively for confirmation, for the Church teaches that without confirmation the grace of baptism and the Eucharist is not complete.

You may be aware that the celebration of confirmation has changed many times over the centuries and even over the past few decades. For example, the age for being confirmed has varied from century to century and even from diocese to diocese or parish to parish. The way the sacrament is viewed and conferred has shifted depending on culture, practical and pastoral needs, and the insights of theologians and religious educators.

What has remained constant, however, is the essence of confirmation. This special, "once-in-a-lifetime" sacrament is designed to deepen our relationship with Christ and his Church and to celebrate the presence and action of the Holy Spirit within us and within the Church.

Confirmation harkens back to the original experience of Pentecost, when the Holy Spirit came down on the infant Church and empowered it to carry on the life and mission of Jesus. Confirmation is our personal Pentecost.

As a sponsor, you will journey with the candidate as he or she prepares to celebrate the sacrament of confirmation. You will help guide him or her in learning what it means to be a confirmed Catholic. Your role as sponsor is a unique opportunity to share your faith with someone directly. Enjoy the experience. Listen to what God is telling you about your own Christian commitment that you ratified at your confirmation, even if it was many years ago.

Don't be afraid. The same Spirit who will come to your candidate in a special way at confirmation is with you as guide and helper. With the Spirit's grace and power at work in you, you will be able to help form your candidate into a committed, active and enthusiastic disciple of Jesus—someone who lives by Gospel values and promotes God's kingdom in the world.

Throughout these sacred days of preparation, let your frequent prayer be "Come, Holy Spirit!"

I heard the voice of the Lord saying, "Whom shall I send? Who will go for us?" "Here I am;" I said; "send me!"

Isaiah 6:8

Initiation by Fire

People become members of many organizations or groups through a period of formation followed by a ritual of acceptance. This is the case for fraternities and sororities, groups such as the Knights of Columbus, religious communities, the military, and even social clubs. The Church is no different.

Initiation into the Church is accomplished by three sacraments: baptism, confirmation and Eucharist. A sacrament is an encounter with Christ in a ritual during which God actually acts *through* symbols to bring about what the symbols stand for. Human beings like rituals and symbols. We mark significant events and express our thoughts and feelings through actions, words and concrete signs. Think, for example, of how we celebrate the birthdays of loved ones. We have parties, give presents, light candles, sing "Happy

Birthday to You," make wishes, blow out the candles, and then eat cake and ice cream.

In sacraments, ordinary things like water, wine, oil, bread, gestures and words express spiritual realities that are invisible. And not only do these symbols point to these realities, they actually bring them into being when they are used in one of our sacramental rituals. This is exactly what happens in baptism, confirmation and the Eucharist.

Three Sacraments of Initiation

Baptism, the first sacrament of initiation, uses water and the words "I baptize you in the name of the Father, and of the Son, and of the Holy Spirit" as its symbols. Water is associated with cleansing and life. At baptism the child you are sponsoring was united with Jesus' saving death and resurrection. Sin was "washed away," and he or she was flooded with new divine life, becoming a child of God and a temple of the Trinity, with a right to the other sacraments.

In confirmation, God again acts to save. This time the symbols are the laying on of hands and the anointing with chrism (holy oil). At confirmation the gifts the Spirit brings are intensified in the recipient. He or she receives more grace to live as Jesus did. As the name of the sacrament suggests, a person's baptism and membership in the Church are "confirmed" in a real and permanent way. Depending on your candidate's age and maturity, confirmation is also an opportunity for him or her to profess the faith personally and publicly and to accept an increased responsibility to live it faithfully.

The third sacrament of initiation is the Eucharist, which uses bread and wine as its symbols. Sharing in this sacrificial meal as Jesus commanded at the Last Supper is the culmination of Christian initiation. Only full members of the Church are invited to it. (In fact, in the early Church those at Mass who were preparing for initiation left after the Word was proclaimed and before the liturgy of the Eucharist.) Through partaking of the Body and Blood of Jesus, the child is united with him and with the other members of the Church.

Baptism by the Holy Spirit

The sacrament of confirmation is foreshadowed in Scripture.

Jesus told Nicodemus that we enter the kingdom of God by being "born of water and Spirit" (John 3:5). Sacramentally, we are born of water through our baptism and we are born of Spirit through our confirmation.

Water and the Spirit played a part when Jesus was baptized by John in the River Jordan and assumed his mission as Messiah. As Jesus came up from the water, the Spirit came down on him in the form of a dove (see Mark 1:9–11). Returning to Nazareth, his hometown, Jesus went to the synagogue and read from the book of the prophet Isaiah:

> The Spirit of the Lord is upon me,
> because he has anointed me
> to bring glad tidings to the poor.
> He has sent me to proclaim liberty to captives
> and recovery of sight to the blind,

to let the oppressed go free,
and to proclaim a year ac-
ceptable to the Lord.
(Luke 4:18-19)

After the reading, Jesus said, "Today this scripture passage is fulfilled
in your hearing" (Luke 4:21).

The Spirit helped Jesus carry out
his mission. At the Last Supper
Jesus promised his followers that he
would ask the Father to send the
Holy Spirit to be their helper too.
Later, on Easter night, Jesus appeared to his apostles and said, "As
the Father has sent me, so I send
you" (John 20:21). He breathed on
them and said, "Receive the holy
Spirit" (John 20:22). And just before he ascended to the Father,
Jesus promised his followers that
they would be baptized with the holy
Spirit and be his witnesses to the
ends of the earth (see Acts 1:1-8).

The Pentecost Event

Jesus was true to his word. On Pentecost, which was originally a Jewish harvest feast, the apostles, Mary
and other followers were gathered
in prayer in an upper room in
Jerusalem. The Holy Spirit came
down on them: "And suddenly there
came from the sky a noise like a
strong driving wind, and it filled the
entire house in which they were.
Then there appeared to them
tongues as of fire, which parted and
came to rest on each one of them.
And they were all filled with the holy
Spirit and began to speak in different tongues, as the Spirit enabled
them to proclaim" (Acts 2:2-4).

Pentecost is sometimes called "the
birthday of the Church." It is the first
time that Jesus' followers were recognized as a group. Filled with the
Spirit, St. Peter, no longer in fear for

his life, went out from the house and boldly witnessed to Jesus. He said, "Repent and be baptized, every one of you, in the name of Jesus Christ for the forgiveness of your sins; and you will receive the gift of the holy Spirit" (Acts 2:38). As a result, three thousand people were baptized that day, and the coming of the Spirit has continued up to the present time— even to the upcoming confirmation of the child you are sponsoring!

Confirmation as a New Pentecost

When your candidate is confirmed, the Holy Spirit most likely won't appear as tongues of flame. The child probably won't begin speaking in tongues either. You might not even notice a big difference in his or her behavior.

Still, faith teaches us that there is a real change that is brought about by the reception of this sacrament. In the child's heart a quiet fire will begin to glow. He or she will experience an increase in the grace needed to continue formation as a good Christian, to witness to Jesus, and to cope with life's challenges.

Years from now, perhaps as a single adult or as a parent, the young person you sponsor will realize that he or she is "suddenly" on fire with love for God and neighbor and become both willing and able to spread the Good News that the kingdom of God has already begun in his or her heart. This is the promise of confirmation as a "new" Pentecost.

Make ready for the Spirit
whose smile—like lightning—sets
free the song of everlasting glory
that now sleeps in your paper
flesh like dynamite.

Thomas Merton

What Is the Sponsor's Role?

Those of us in religious education hope that the days are gone when a godparent or confirmation sponsor merely says, "Yes, I'd be honored," makes an appearance at the sacrament, and then disappears from the candidate's life.

The Church is taking the roles of godparent and confirmation sponsor much more seriously today. Being a sponsor will require a big commitment from you: It will involve sharing your personal faith.

After reading this chapter, you may wonder if you can fill such an important bill. But don't worry. There are people to help you (the parish confirmation team and the parents), and this book will give you some practical information and ideas.

The best way to look at it is that the time and effort required of you as a sponsor will not only benefit your candidate. You will feel good about yourself, grow in faith, and maybe even have some fun.

Job Description

As a sponsor you will serve as a mentor, role model, and friend for someone being admitted to full communion with the Catholic Church. Whether the candidate is a younger child or a teenager, you are being asked to assist his or her parents in fostering their child's spiritual growth. Your main job is to show that a confirmed person (which you are) should act as a true witness to Christ and fulfill the obligations assumed through the sacraments of initiation.

You may already be your candidate's godparent. Nowadays god-parents are often the preferred sponsors, because they are already responsible for the spiritual development of the candidate.

Genders need not match. A man may serve as a sponsor for a girl or woman, and a woman may be a sponsor for a boy or man.

Ideally you will be able to:

• meet several times with your candidate;

• participate in preparation activities;

• come to one or two pre-confirmation meetings;

• attend the rehearsal;

• at confirmation, stand behind the candidate before the bishop. (If necessary, someone may stand in for you. You will still be recorded as the official sponsor.)

Requirements

In order to fulfill this role, a sponsor needs to meet certain qualifications. In fact, you may be asked to secure a certificate of recommendation from your home parish. If any of the following does not describe you, make it known to the persons who asked you to be a sponsor.

(On the other hand, if you feel that you haven't been the greatest Catholic but are willing to change your ways and try harder, this could be the perfect opportunity to get yourself "right" with the Church and with God. If you are in this situation, see a priest, either at your own parish or at the one at which you have been asked to be a sponsor.

He will help you do what you need to do to be a good sponsor.)

To be a sponsor you do not have to be a perfect saint or even an outstanding Catholic, just someone who believes in Jesus and tries to live his way of love. One of the most valuable things you might share with your candidate is your own weakness in following Jesus. This is reality—Catholics sometimes fail. We know, though, that we can always trust in the loving mercy of Jesus.

In essence, a sponsor has a vocation to be a companion to someone on a faith journey. You will serve much like the angel Raphael, who guided the young man Tobiah (see the Book of Tobit), or like Naomi, who mentored her daughter-in-law Ruth (see the Book of Ruth).

According to the rules of the Church, a sponsor must:

• be a member of the Catholic Church who is fully initiated by baptism, confirmation, and the Eucharist;

• be a mature person at least sixteen years old;

• be in good standing with the Church;

• be willing to share the faith with the candidate;

• be an example of good Christian living.

Ideally, a sponsor should live close enough and be available to help prepare the candidate for confirmation, although this is not an absolute rule. It is more important that he or she has a listening ear and a caring heart!

✺

Y ou, eternal Trinity, are a deep
sea: the more I enter you, the
more I discover, the more I seek.

St. Catherine of Siena

❧

The Holy Spirit, the Paraclete

A priest once posed a trick question to a class of youngsters. He asked, "Who is the oldest Person in the Trinity?" One lad answered, "The Father?" A second child guessed, "The Son?" A third child responded, "The Holy Spirit?" After replying no to all three answers, Father said, "Doesn't anyone know who the oldest is?" A timid voice ventured, "Is *Amen* the oldest?" (The answer, of course, is that all three persons of the Trinity are exactly the same age, since all have existed for all eternity.)

Many Catholics are as unsure about the Trinity as that class was. And the Person of the Trinity who is most mysterious and misunderstood is the Holy Spirit, partly because the Spirit is not visualized as a human being as Jesus—and to a lesser extent the Father—are. People often pray to the Father and to the Son, for example, but seldom to the Holy Spirit. This is ironic because the Holy Spirit is the one who is specially sent to be our "Paraclete," our advocate, defender and comforter. (Other images for the Holy Spirit are "the Breath of God" and "the Finger of God's Right Hand.")

God the Holy Spirit

Although the Holy Spirit is often depicted in art as a dove, the Spirit is definitely not a bird. The Holy Spirit has equal power with the other Persons in the Trinity and like them is eternal (having no beginning and no end). At Sunday Mass we pray in the Creed, "I believe in the Holy Spirit, the Lord, the giver of life, who proceeds from the Father and the Son."

Theologians suggest that the Holy Spirit is the "personification" of the love between the Father and the Son. Although the three Persons are one and do everything together, we assign them tasks. We credit the Father with creation, the Son with redemption, and the Spirit with sanctification. In other words, the Spirit's chief role to is make us holy, to make us more "God-like" or more "like Christ" (which is the definition of what it means to be a Christian).

The Spirit's Role in Salvation

The Spirit first appears in Scripture at the dawn of creation: "In the beginning, when God created the heavens and the earth, the earth was a formless wasteland, and darkness covered the abyss, while a mighty wind swept over the waters" (Genesis 1:1–2). The wind is literally the Spirit of God, the Spirit who brings forth all life.

This same Spirit inspired the prophets and other Scripture writers to speak and write what God wanted made known, which we call "divine revelation."

When our loving God decided to save humanity from sin and death, the life-giving Holy Spirit acted again. After the Angel Gabriel told the Virgin Mary that she would be the Mother of God, she asked how this could be. Gabriel explained: "The holy Spirit will come upon you, and the power of the Most High will overshadow you. Therefore the child to be born will be called holy, the Son of God" (Luke 1:35). Thus it was the Spirit who miraculously brought about the Incarnation, the mystery of God becoming man. Later, when Mary visited her relative Elizabeth, Luke's Gospel says

that Elizabeth, "filled with the holy Spirit" (Luke 1:41), greeted Mary as "the mother of my Lord" (Luke 1:43).

After his baptism, "Filled with the holy Spirit, Jesus returned from the Jordan and was led by the Spirit into the desert" (Luke 4:1). There he was tempted by the devil, and afterwards he began teaching with such power that he soon won the esteem of all. The Spirit also enabled Jesus to work miracles, to heal, to forgive, and to redeem. Jesus told his disciples, "The Advocate, the holy Spirit that the Father will send in my name—he will teach you everything and remind you of all that [I] told you" (John 14:26).

After Jesus ascended to heaven, the Father sent the Spirit to be our guide and our helper. In the Bible, the book of the Acts of the Apostles (which is about the early Church) is sometimes called "the Book of the Holy Spirit" because it refers to the Spirit's action so often.

Finally, Jesus is with us in the Eucharist through his Spirit. At Mass the priest prays that the Spirit's action may transform the bread and wine: "And so, Father, we bring you these gifts. We ask you to make them holy by the power of your Spirit, that they may become the body and blood of your Son, our Lord Jesus Christ" (Eucharistic Prayer III).

Role in the Life of the Child You Are Sponsoring

The Spirit empowers your candidate to follow Jesus and to love, spread and defend our faith. Whenever the child has the impulse to do good, it is the Spirit who is at work. Whenever he or she is inspired, it is the Spirit. Just as promptly as the child might excuse faults by saying, "The devil made me do it," after good deeds he or she could acknowledge, "The Spirit made me do it!"

You might encourage the child you are sponsoring to be open to the Spirit. This means to listen to God and to be sensitive to God's grace and action in our hearts. Explain that to do these things we must be quiet and prayerful. You might point out to the child times when the Spirit is at work in his or her life. For example, maybe he or she does a chore after being told to do so only once or shares something with another person without being asked. You can comment, "I saw that you were listening to the Holy Spirit in your heart."

The Spirit does not only make us personally holy but also works through us to transform the whole world into God's kingdom of peace and justice. The Spirit is the source of unity and love among people, in particular among church members. No wonder the Church celebrates the mystery of the Spirit in a separate sacrament!

Symbols of the Spirit

On the first Pentecost, fire and wind heralded the Spirit's presence. The Spirit is likened to these two natural forces because of their qualities and uses.

Fire is beautiful, powerful, mysterious and helpful. It enables us to see, just like the Spirit enlightens us to see truths. Fire also purifies and refines, just as the Spirit can burn away our faults and sins to make us pure like God. When fire touches most things, it turns them into fire too. When the Spirit comes in contact with us, we become holy like God.

Wind is also a good symbol for the Spirit. It is invisible like God. Wind can be a strong gale and create changes, or it can be a cool, refreshing breeze. Similarly the Spirit can blow forcefully in our lives or can be gentle and soothing.

It is said that the world has experienced first the age of the Father and then the age of the Son. Now we are in the age of the Holy Spirit.

Holy Spirit, Spirit of truth, you are the reward of the saints, the comforter of souls, light in the darkness, riches to the poor, treasure to lovers, food for the hungry, comfort to those who are wandering; to sum up, you are the one in whom all treasures are contained.

St. Mary Magdalene de Pazzi

The Spirit's Gifts and Fruits

After his or her confirmation, the child likely will receive gifts from family and friends—including a special gift from you, the sponsor. God—the supreme gift-giver—is not to be outdone, however.

The Spirit is God's gift to the Church, and the sacrament of confirmation is God's gift to each one of us. What's more, the Spirit arrives with gifts for those who are being confirmed. Actually, the child you are sponsoring received these gifts when the Spirit first came at baptism. At confirmation, they are sharpened and heightened.

First, the Spirit brings the theological virtues of faith, hope and charity. These virtues help direct the child's life to God. The Spirit also brings the cardinal moral virtues of prudence, justice, fortitude and temperance.

These virtues undergird moral life as a whole and help the child act the right way. In addition to these seven virtues, the Spirit empowers the child with seven supernatural habits called "the gifts of the Holy Spirit," which were prophetically foreshadowed in Isaiah 11:2-3. At confirmation there will be a great outpouring of these seven gifts.

The Gifts Described

The fact that there are seven gifts is symbolic. Seven is a lucky number! For the Jewish people it stood for perfection and wholeness. The Spirit's seven gifts equip the child to live a full and happy Christian life.

The first four gifts of the Spirit enable us to know God's will. The other three help us to do it. The names of the gifts listed here are those used today in the rite of con-firmation. Their old names are in parentheses.

Wisdom enables us to see all things as God sees them—in relation to salvation. It helps us to love the things of God and to recognize the true worth of persons, events and things. Wisdom keeps us focused on God's will and God's plan for us.

Examples: If the child is wise, he or she will value life in all its forms. He or she will appreciate the sacrament of confirmation!

Understanding helps us grasp the meaning and the consequences of the truths of the faith. The Spirit enlightens us to penetrate mysteries like the Trinity, the Eucharist and the cross. The way the child lives is the litmus test for true understanding (not just his or her ability to give back information). The child will grow in understanding through prayer and reading the Bible.

Example: The child shows reverence for the Eucharist by genuflecting and by being quiet before the Blessed Sacrament.

Right judgment (counsel) helps us to make decisions by seeking advice and by being open to good advice. This gift also helps us to guide others to a good decision. You can assist the child in making good decisions. Teach him or her to think, pray, seek advice, and be free from the influence of prejudice, passions, selfishness and purely human standards.

Example: The child may choose friends wisely.

Knowledge helps us to see God in all things, to know ourselves, and to know the teachings of Jesus. Learning about Jesus and his Church deepens knowledge.

Example: The child gives evidence of knowledge when the sight of a beautiful sunset or the ocean leads him or her to think of the Creator.

Courage (fortitude) gives us the inner strength to do what is right, to stand up for our faith, and to keep on living the Gospel values—especially in hard times. You can serve as a model of courage for the child you are sponsoring.

Example: The child shows courage by taking an unpopular stand because of our faith and by not succumbing to peer pressure.

Reverence (piety) helps us think of ourselves as children of God and be eager to serve God. It leads us to love and worship God and to respect all God's creatures. It makes us pray with love and confidence.

Examples: How the child prays and how he or she treats siblings and friends reveal the degree to which this gift is present.

Wonder and awe (fear of the Lord) helps us to realize God's power and majesty and our total dependence on God. With this gift, we marvel at God and God's love for us. Because of these sentiments in our heart, we dread displeasing God.

Example: A sign of this gift is that the child is quick to ask God's forgiveness after sin.

Other Gifts

After Pentecost the apostles spoke in tongues. People who were gathered from all nations for the feast could understand their language. The Spirit sometimes bestows special gifts, or *charisms,* on individual church members for the good of all. In 1 Corinthians 12:7–11 is a list of some of these charismatic gifts: healing, prophecy, speaking in tongues and interpretation of tongues, miracles, discernment of spirits, and faith. Don't expect the child to exhibit all these gifts. On the other hand, don't be surprised if they show up someday in ways you least expect!

Fruits of the Spirit

Those who live by the Spirit and make use of the Spirit's gifts are characterized by what are known as "the fruits of the Spirit." Nine of these virtues are listed in Galatians 5:22-23. All of these qualities are forms of love. The twelve fruits of the Holy Spirit are listed on the opposite page:

The Fruits of the Holy Spirit

1. charity

2. faith (fidelity)

3. joy

4. modesty

5. benignity (generosity, kindness)

6. goodness

7. peace

8. patience

9. continence (self-control)

10. chastity

11. endurance (long-suffering)

12. mildness

By the sacrament of confirmation, [the baptized] are more perfectly bound to the Church and are enriched with a special strength of the Holy Spirit. Hence they are, as true witnesses of Christ, more strictly obliged to spread and defend the faith by word and deed.

Second Vatican Council
Constitution on the Church

Confirmation's Symbols

We humans surround significant events with rituals and symbols. Take a wedding. We celebrate a couple's new life together with beautiful clothes, flowers, music, processions, receptions and showers, gifts, often a Mass, and especially by the exchange of vows. The new life of Christ celebrated in confirmation is also accompanied by rituals and symbols that express what is actually happening inside those receiving the sacrament.

Through the centuries, the recognized ritual by which confirmation is actually conferred has alternated between the symbols of the imposition of hands and the anointing with oil. Today's rite incorporates both. The individual laying on of hands occurs simultaneously with the anointing.

The Bishop

In most ordinary circumstances, the bishop of the diocese or one of his auxiliary bishops administers the sacrament of confirmation. A priest may help confirm when there are large groups, and in some special situations a priest can administer the sacrament himself. This may happen when converts are being received into the Church at the Easter Vigil, for example, or when someone is in danger of death.

The presence of a bishop underscores the importance of what is occurring. It also gives the candidates an opportunity to meet one of the local leaders of the Church to which they are more fully binding themselves.

It is also fitting that a bishop confirms, because he is a successor of the apostles upon whom the Holy Spirit descended on Pentecost. Because the bishop is a leader of the Church, his presence expresses the union of the new Christian with the broader Church. Even if a priest confirms, a bishop is always present in the sense that the chrism used in confirmation has always been consecrated by a bishop that liturgical year on Holy Thursday.

Laying on of Hands

Touch is a powerful sign. Think of caresses, handshakes, pats on the back. Even more powerful is the formal imposition or laying on of hands. In the Old Testament, the laying on of hands was a sign of special blessing or commissioning. In the New Testament, Jesus often touched people as he healed them: a leper, Peter's mother-in-law, a blind man, Jairus's daughter, the bent-over woman. The apostles imposed hands to confer authority, as is still done today in the ordination of priests and bishops. They also laid hands on the Samaritans to give them the Holy Spirit (see Acts of the Apostles 8:14–17).

Chrism

Chrism is olive (or plant) oil mixed with balsam (or perfume). On Holy Thursday each year, the bishop consecrates chrism at a special Chrism Mass. It is then distributed to each parish in the diocese. Anointing with oil sets someone apart for a special mission. The Hebrews anointed their kings, priests and prophets, for example, and anointing is part of all ordination ceremonies in the Church.

The Eastern churches actually call the sacrament of confirmation "chrismation." The word *chrism* is from the Greek word for "anointed." *Christ* means "the anointed one." He was king, priest and prophet—all rolled into one. In confirmation, your son or daughter will be anointed for these same three roles in carrying out Christ's mission:

• Confirmed Christians are *royalty,* nothing less than sons and daughters of almighty God.

• Confirmed Christians are *priests* who intercede for people and offer prayers and sacrifices to God.

• Confirmed Christians are *prophets* who are not afraid to speak God's word, especially when it isn't popular.

Clearly oil is a good symbol for the Spirit. Consider how oil enhances our lives. There is bath oil, suntan lotion, baby oil, oil that soothes aching muscles and smooths skin, oil that makes athletes' bodies limber and glistening, oil that heals, oil that starts fires, and oil that helps cook our food. As the scent of the sacred chrism permeates the church, it reminds all that the candidates for confirmation are to take the fragrance of Christ into the world. (See the prayer of John Henry Cardinal Newman on page 74.)

The Sign of the Cross

The cross the bishop traces on the child's forehead is the sign of a Christian, the sign of Christ. The child was redeemed by the suffering, death and resurrection of Jesus. Followers of Christ share his cross and endure suffering for his sake. The cross recalls Jesus' suffering but also his victory. It is our insignia as confirmed Christians.

Confirmation Name

People are often named for someone: a grandparent, aunt or uncle, historical figure or popular celebrity. As the child joined the family of God at baptism, he or she may well have been named after a saint as well. That saint may have become the child's inspiration.

Names given later in life often signify a change in status. When God called Abraham and Sarah, for example, he changed their names. Jesus changed the apostle Simon's name to Peter. Vowed religious sometimes take new names. When a woman marries, she often assumes her husband's last name (or sometimes they both adopt hyphenated joint last names).

For this next stage of initiation, the child you are sponsoring has a choice: either to keep his or her baptismal name (to make clear that confirmation seals the baptismal commitment) or to take an additional name. The only requirement is that the confirmation name should be that of a canonized saint or biblical figure or at least someone who has been beatified by the Church, such as Blessed Mother Teresa.

"Be Sealed"

As the bishop confirms the child, he will say, "[Name], be sealed with the Gift of the Holy Spirit." These words are an ancient formula adopted from the Byzantine rite. A seal is a sign of identification and authenticity. Formerly letters and documents were sealed with the imprint of a person's seal or imprint ring pressed into hot wax. During confirmation God seals candidates as his own.

This spiritual seal, or character, is permanent. Confirmation is a once-in-a-lifetime sacrament. It signifies that we belong totally to Christ and are in his service.

❀

Before you, Father,

In righteousness and humility,

With you, Brother,

In faith and courage,

In you, Spirit,

In stillness.

Dag Hammarskjöld

❀

The Rite of Confirmation

You might be old enough to remember confirmation as the time for becoming "soldiers of Christ," when the focus was on the gift of *fortitude*. During the ceremony the bishop "slapped" candidates on the cheek. This signified that they were ready to undergo hardships in defense of the faith and even to bear witness by martyrdom. Nothing caused more pre-confirmation jitters and nervous giggles than the symbolic tap.

We now see confirmation as not so much a rite of passage or sacrament of witness but a step toward full initiation in the faith. Elements of the various views of the sacrament linger, but today's emphasis is on developing a deeper relationship with Jesus and his Church. That is why confirmation is administered ideally in the context of the Eucharist, at the time when the people of God are gathered to hear the word of God and share his Body and Blood.

Presentation of the Candidates

After the gospel is read, the priest or catechetical leader presents the candidates to the bishop for confirmation. They are called by name or as a group to enter the sanctuary or to stand in place. This signifies the candidates desire to live as Christians. Then everyone is seated, and the bishop gives a homily. Very often, the bishop will quiz the candidates at random about their knowledge of the faith. This is usually done with gentleness and good spirits, recognizing how self-conscious young people can be. The bishop will then ask the pastor and the religious educators to attest that the candidates have in fact received the proper instruction and are ready to be confirmed.

Renewal of Baptismal Vows

The candidates stand and renew their baptismal promises thereby committing themselves anew to Christ. This renewal links this second sacrament of initiation with the first one, which is baptism.

The bishop asks, "Do you reject Satan and all his works and all his empty promises?" The candidates respond, "I do." Then the bishop asks if they believe the different truths of the Catholic faith listed on the opposite page. After each question, the candidates answer, "I do."

Do you believe in:

- God, the Father almighty, creator of heaven and earth?

- Jesus Christ, his only Son, our Lord, who was born of the Virgin Mary, was crucified, died and was buried, rose from the dead, and is now seated at the right hand of the Father?

- the Holy Spirit, the Lord, the giver of life, who came upon the apostles at Pentecost and today is given to you sacramentally in confirmation?

- the holy catholic church, the communion of saints?

- the forgiveness of sins, the resurrection of the body, and life everlasting?

Prayer Over the Candidates

The bishop invites everyone to pray to the Father "that he will pour out the Holy Spirit to strengthen his sons and daughters with his gifts and anoint them to be more like Christ."

After this prayer, the bishop and any priests who will administer the sacrament with him extend their hands over all the candidates. The bishop then prays:

> All-powerful God, Father of
>   our Lord Jesus Christ,
> by water and the Holy Spirit
> you freed your sons and
>   daughters from sin
> and gave them new life.
> Send your Holy Spirit upon
>   them
> to be their Helper and Guide.
> Give them the spirit of wis-
>   dom and understanding,

> the spirit of right judgment
>   and courage,
> the spirit of knowledge and
>   reverence.
> Fill them with the spirit of
>   wonder and awe in your
>   presence.
> We ask this through Christ
>   our Lord.

Confirmation Itself

The actual confirmation takes place when the bishop lays his hand on each candidate's head and anoints him or her with chrism.

The child you are sponsoring will walk up to the bishop with you. You will place your hand on the child's right shoulder. Either the child or you will state the confirmation name and hand the bishop or his assistant a card with this name on it. The bishop will then trace the Sign of the Cross with chrism on the candidate's forehead, saying, "[Name], be sealed with the Gift of the Holy Spirit." The child will respond, "Amen."

(In the Byzantine rite, different parts of the body are anointed and with each anointing the words "the seal of the gift of the holy Spirit" are said.)

Then the bishop will offer a sign of peace. He will probably shake the child's hand and maybe yours as well and may say, "Peace be with you." You should respond, "And also with you."

After the sacrament is conferred, Mass continues as usual. The child will receive the Eucharist—the third of the sacraments of initiation—with the rest of the congregation. The Mass concludes, fittingly, with a special blessing over all the people that they may have courage to spread the Good News of Jesus as confirmed Christians.

The love of God has been poured out into our hearts through the holy Spirit that has been given to us.

Romans 5:5

The Evolution of Confirmation

There is an old joke among priests and religious educators that goes something like this: "Do you know how we get rid of bats in the church belfry? We confirm them, and then they go away and never come back."

This joke is a sad commentary on what the sacrament of confirmation has become for many people. No longer is it an initiation rite that inserts a young person more deeply into the life of the Church. Instead confirmation is seen by some parents and sponsors as the final step of a young person's religious formation. After confirmation, it is often assumed, young people are finished with formal religious education (and many of them with going to Mass regularly as well).

How did confirmation come to be regarded as a rite of passage that concluded one's formal instruction? Why is there a movement today to have children confirmed before their First Communion? The sacrament's history contains the answers.

In the Early Church

At first catechumens (those desiring to be Christian) were initiated into the faith community during the Easter Vigil in one grand liturgy that included all three sacraments of initiation. (This is still the practice now for converts and is very moving to observe.) The catechumens were rubbed with oil. They descended into a pool where the local bishop immersed them and baptized them. They ascended, were clothed with a white robe, and experienced the laying on of hands and anointing by the bishop. Then they proceeded to places of honor where they participated in the Eucharist for the first time. Thus, Christian initiation consisted of one event with several initiatory moments.

Growth Brings Change

Not until the Lateran Council of 1215 was confirmation clearly defined as a separate sacrament. The separation occurred for practical and pastoral reasons. In the fourth century, the Emperor Constantine had proclaimed Christianity to be the state religion, resulting in large numbers of adult baptisms. A little later, St. Augustine's teachings on original sin encouraged the practice of baptizing infants to ensure that they went to heaven if they died. These two developments made it practically impossible for bishops to initiate every Christian personally with the sacraments of baptism, confirmation and Eucharist.

The bishops of the Eastern Church solved the problem by delegating the entire initiation ceremony to priests, reserving for themselves only the blessing of the oil. To this day the Eastern Churches initiate with all three sacraments at once. A baby baptized at an Eastern Church receives a drop of wine for the Eucharist and is confirmed at the same time.

The bishops of the West also delegated to priests the initiation ceremony of baptizing and anointing with chrism. However, they retained for themselves the final anointing or laying on of hands. Whenever the bishops visited a region, they would anoint or lay hands on all the newly-baptized there. The West developed this sealing part of initiation into a separate ceremony that evolved

into the sacrament of confirmation, a sacrament that confirmed the baptized in the faith.

A Shift in Theology

In the Middle Ages, it became the practice to confirm close to adolescence instead of at infancy. Confirmation became known as the sacrament of maturity (much like the Jewish ceremonies of Bar Mitzvah and Bat Mitzvah). Those who received confirmation were considered old enough to begin living active, responsible Christian lives. At confirmation the Christian was sealed as a witness for Christ and fortified by an increase of the Spirit's gifts to fight, suffer and die for the faith. A bishop named Faustus introduced the notion that the sacrament made a person a "soldier of Christ." This idea took hold, and the sign of peace was even replaced by a gentle slap on the face to indicate readiness for life's battles.

Many of us who prepare candidates for confirmation welcome the return to the stress on initiation rather than on maturity. We know (as do many parents and sponsors) that most of our young Christians are not completely mature by the date of confirmation (even if it is done in high school). We certainly know that they will not instantly become mature when the sacrament is conferred. Conversion to Christ is a gradual process, in which confirmation is but one sacramental milestone.

Change in Order

Confirmation used to precede First Communion. This way confirmation was easily seen as a step to full celebration with the community at Eucharist. Then in 1910, Pope Pius X made it possible for seven-year-olds to receive Communion, and confirmation became for many the last sacrament of initiation to be celebrated. Where this is still the case, confirmation's role of leading to the Eucharist must be emphasized in ways other than chronological.

The RCIA Model

The Second Vatican Council called for a restoration of what is called the *catechumenate*, a formation program for new Christians. This gave birth to the Rite of Christian Initiation of Adults (RCIA), which guides perspective members of the Church to see Christianity as a way of life.

The RCIA stresses the involvement of the community in the preparation of the candidates. It includes rites throughout the preparation

period, such as the Rite of Enroll-
ment. Some confirmation programs
for youth incorporate the principles
and the process of the RCIA. If the
child you are sponsoring is in such
a program, he or she will be the
richer for it.

Every time we say, "I believe in
the Holy Spirit," we mean that we
believe there is a living God able
and willing to enter human
personality and change it.

J.B. Phillips

How Can You Help Prepare the Child You Are Sponsoring?

You have been asked to be a helper in preparing the young candidate for confirmation. This is first and foremost the parents' job, but you can work closely with them by planning and carrying out the activities suggested here. Some projects they might do alone; others they might pass on to you; some you might do together with them.

Although you may not always think so, the values and attitudes exhibited by the adults in their lives deeply impress children. The daily living and example of parents, friends and relatives have been a primary preparation for the sacrament of confirmation throughout the life of the child you are sponsoring. Adult exhortations to do good and avoid evil, to make Sunday Eucharist and prayer a priority, to practice generosity, integrity, selflessness and love have been one of the factors that have helped form the young candidate into a Christian.

In the months before confirmation, you might initiate or renew your efforts to help nurture the child's spiritual growth. Arrange to meet with the candidate before the confirmation so you can get to know each other better and begin to talk about your faith. Invite the child to your home or go out to dinner together.

Following are some suggestions for immediate preparation for this sacrament.

Attend Preparation Sessions

Parishes usually have pre-confirmation meetings for parents. Do your best to attend, if sponsors are welcome. It will give you insights into the sacrament and ideas for assisting the child. Go to the confirmation rehearsal as well.

Help make sure that the child is present for lessons and for special preparation events such as a Retreat Day or a Spirit Day. Offer to drive if needed, or do something to indicate your support, such as sending a note or taking the child out to lunch before or after the event.

Reinforce Lessons and Choice of Name

Talk to the child about what he or she is learning about confirmation. Share material from this book. Tell him or her about your own confirmation: what it meant to you, how you felt, who your sponsor was, what your confirmation name was, and why you chose that name.

The child will be asked to choose a confirmation name. He or she may choose to use the baptismal name or pick a new one. In either case, you can help the candidate research the meaning of the name and information about the life of the saint by consulting books on the lives of the saints or searching the name on the Internet. Guide the child to have good reasons for the confirmation name chosen. (You might want to check the Web site www.actapublications.com for a free, comprehensive list of biblical and saints' names.)

Call on the Holy Spirit

The Holy Spirit is our silent partner in life. Foster in the child you are sponsoring the habit of turning to the Spirit for help especially at these times:

• when inspiration is needed,

• when faced with a problem,

• when making a decision,

• when he or she is being tempted.

Help Procure Documents

If the child did not receive baptism and First Communion at the parish where confirmation will be administered, he or she will be asked to present a certificate of baptism and verification of First Communion. Offer to help the parents find and procure the necessary documents.

A certificate of recommendation of you from your parish may be also be required. Make sure you get yours in a timely manner and turn it in to the parish where the child is being confirmed.

Help Write to the Bishop

Candidates for confirmation are sometimes encouraged to write to the local bishop. You might help him or her to follow the instructions given for this letter. Check that it is correctly set up and addressed, but let the candidate compose the letter. The letter might:

• contain a statement of faith,

• tell the bishop that he or she is ready for confirmation,

• express a desire to be confirmed,

• give the reasons why he or she would like to be confirmed.

Help Prepare for an Interview

An interview or two with a priest or member of the confirmation team might be held to help assess the child's readiness for the sacrament. It will probably cover three areas:

• *Faith.* Confirmation preparation includes an overview of the faith. Does the child know and understand what he or she is vowing to live by? You can help the candidate by going over the textbook or by discussing the Apostles' Creed.

• *Service.* A Christian loves through actions as Jesus did. Has the child you are sponsoring experienced the meaning of this? Help him or her do service projects, contribute time, talent and treasure to charitable organizations, or simply be a good neighbor to someone.

• *Prayer.* A Christian has a relationship with the Trinity: the Father who created us, the Son who redeemed us, and the Spirit who dwells within us. Does the child try to deepen his or her friendship with God through prayer? Does he or she show appreciation for the Eucharist? You might go together to Sunday Mass and talk about it afterwards.

Participate in Service

As a Christian, the candidate is called to serve others. Some confirmation programs encourage or even require candidates to do service projects or log service hours. Join in the child's experiences by being a chauffeur, working side-by-side at a soup kitchen, helping a neighbor, or carrying out a work of mercy. Read and discuss the Beatitudes with the child (Matthew 5:3–10) and the parable about the works of mercy (Matthew 25:31–46).

Celebrate Reconciliation

Celebrating the sacrament of reconciliation before confirmation is strongly recommended for candidates, and it is an excellent idea for sponsors as well. As the child you are sponsoring prepares to be bound more closely to God and to the community, it is right that he or she asks forgiveness and atones for anything that might have hurt relationships with them. If the program doesn't schedule the sacrament of reconciliation, encourage the child to celebrate this sacrament independently. You might go to confession with him or her for the occasion.

Write a Support Letter

Some confirmation teams ask parents, sponsors, other family members and friends to write support letters to the candidate. These are presented to the candidate before confirmation, often on a retreat or day of reflection. Reading these letters is often a powerful and meaningful experience for the candidates. Even if your confirmation preparation program doesn't ask for these letters, you might write one to the child. The letter could include:

- gifts you and others see in the candidate,

- good deeds the candidate has done,

- the dreams and goals you envision for him or her,

- why you love and appreciate him or her,

- why you rejoice that the candidate will be receiving the sacrament,

- an encouragement to be strong in living out the Catholic faith,

- your promise of prayer and help in the future.

Keep in Touch

Don't let being a confirmation sponsor be a one-time deal. If you act as if this special relationship is a life-long one, so will the child you sponsor. Keep in touch in a variety of ways—seeking the child out at parties you both attend, asking how he or she is doing in school, sending a book or article you read on religion that might be of interest.

One longer-range idea is to put the date of the child's confirmation on your list of anniversaries and special days to be remembered each year. It will blow his or her mind if you send a card or call the child each year on that date, since most likely no one else will remember it. This simple act of remembering the day may help the child recall the commitments he or she made at confirmation.

Four Other Tips

1. Acquaint the child with the bishop of the diocese: his name, where he lives, his contributions to the diocese, his motto and crest. You might visit the cathedral, which is the bishop's official church, participate in Mass there, and tour it together.

2. Take the child to a baptism or to the Easter Vigil services to witness others committing themselves to Jesus Christ.

3. Consider blessing the child when you see him or her. Trace the Sign of the Cross on his or her forehead. You might use holy water if it is easily available, but the key is to make it a quick, friendly, natural gesture between sponsor and child.

4. Give the child a special notebook to use as a journal during the time of preparation for confirmation. In it he or she could write reflections on the stages of preparation for the sacrament, prayers, poems and favorite Scripture quotations. After confirmation mementos can be added, such as photos or cards.

A Final Word

Supported and encouraged by members of the community, and in particular by you and his or her parents, the child you are sponsoring will feel a new sense of belonging to the faith community when he or she is confirmed. Inspired by Christians willing to share their faith, he or she will be drawn to be one with them and desire to enter more deeply into the Church's life of faith, prayer, community and loving service. Then the child will be better prepared to fulfill the Christian's responsibility "to spread and defend the faith both by word and by deed as true witnesses of Christ" (*Constitution on the Church,* #11).

W here the Spirit of God is,
there is the Church.

St. Irenaeus

Questions and Answers

The day of confirmation should be a happy one for your and the child you are sponsoring. The following questions and answers are intended to allay some concerns or fears, add to your understanding, and make the day memorable.

What if I can't make the actual ceremony?

It is possible for you to be present at the sacrament by proxy. Someone can stand in for you at the ceremony. But do make every effort to be there in person if it is at all possible. Remember that confirmation is a once-in-a-lifetime sacrament and that it is a great honor to have been chosen to be a sponsor.

What should I wear?

Those in charge of the confirmation program may provide guidelines for how the sponsors should dress. In view of the special occasion and the public witness that is being made, it is fitting that males wear a sport coat, tie and dress slacks or a suit. Women might wear a nice dress, suit, or pantsuit. The important thing, though, is that the apparel be neat, clean and modest. Keep in mind that this is a special religious celebration.

What would be an appropriate gift?

Gifts are a good idea anytime something special happens, and confirmation is certainly a special occasion. Although a gift of money is nice, a gift that would help the child grow in the spiritual life is a great idea—especially from the sponsor. Some suggestions are the following:

• prayerbook;

• Bible;

• rosary;

• statue, medal or picture of the child's patron saint;

• plaque, key ring, or other object

featuring the child's confirmation name;

- book on the patron saint or some aspect of the faith;

- CD or video of Christian music;

- journaling book;

- statue or picture of Jesus or Mary;

- artwork depicting the Holy Spirit.

Why is the child being confirmed at this age?

This is the hardest and most controversial question surrounding this sacrament. In 2001 the United States Conference of Catholic Bishops stated that "the sacrament of confirmation in the Latin Rite shall be conferred between the age of discretion [seven years] and about 16 years of age." There are different schools of thought as to the best age for confirmation. Those who emphasize the graces conferred by the sacrament argue "the sooner the better." They realize that children could use the Spirit's special help during the preteen years. Other people view the sacrament as a rite of passage that marks spiritual adulthood. They prefer to confirm later. Those who wish to reestablish the correct order in the sacraments of initiation are putting confirmation before First Communion. Still others would like to see confirmation reunited with baptism.

As a result of these different philosophies, the sacrament is administered at various ages in parishes throughout the world. The best thing for you to do is to enter enthusiastically into the local practice and to get as much out of it as you and the candidate can at the age it is celebrated in the child's parish.

What happens after confirmation?

In the RCIA, which is for adults joining the Church or being confirmed, after the initiation at the Easter Vigil there is a five-week period called *mystagogy*. During this time the new Christians attempt to make their faith a vibrant part of their lives. They pray, deepen their knowledge and practice of the faith, and perform acts of charity.

Even if the child you are sponsoring doesn't experience this formal post-confirmation practice, something akin to it would certainly be beneficial. It is important that the child understands that the faith he or she was so focused on during confirmation should grow. The good spiritual practices assumed during the preparation period need to continue: prayer, Sunday Eucharist, penance, acts of charity and service, and involvement with the parish. After the sacrament, your encouragement and example are still needed, maybe even more. You should continue your interest in and support of the child's spiritual formation in some way. Confirmation is not an end to our spiritual journey but a supernatural boost on that journey.

Scripture Readings for Confirmation

You have helped prepare for the upcoming confirmation by reading this book. Another way you can prepare is to read and ponder the following Scripture passages related to this sacrament. Arrange some private time to read a passage. Then consider what it means to you and your life. Let your thoughts give rise to resolutions that will help you be a better sponsor during the preparation period and afterwards. You may record your resolutions on page 71. Every now and then, read your resolutions and review how you are keeping them.

Joel 3:1–2 (God promises to pour out his spirit on the human race.)

Ezekiel 37:1–14 (Dry bones are brought to life though God's spirit.)

Matthew 5:3–11 (The beatitudes are a guideline for Christian life.)

Matthew 22:34–39 (The greatest commandments are to love.)

Matthew 25:14–30 (We are to use our gifts.)

Matthew 25:31–46 (Works of mercy for others are done for Jesus.)

John 3:1–15 (Jesus tells Nicodemus about birth by the spirit.)

Romans 8:14 (Those who are led by the spirit of God are children of God.)

Galatians 4:6 (The spirit of Jesus in us cries out, "Abba, Father.")

Luke 24:49 (When the Spirit comes, the apostles will be clothed with power from on high.)

Romans 8:11 (We will rise from the dead through the Spirit of Jesus who dwells in us.)

Ephesians 1:11–14 (Our sealing with the holy spirit is the first step to full salvation.)

1 Thessalonians 5:19 (Do not quench the Spirit.)

1 Thessalonians 1:6 (The word of God is received with joy from the Holy Spirit.)

1 Corinthians 2:12–13 (The spirit helps us understand and speak about the things of God.)

1 Corinthians 12:3 (No one can say Jesus is Lord except for the Holy Spirit.)

1 Corinthians 12:4–11 (The Spirit produces different gifts in individuals.)

1 Corinthians 12:12–13 (We are all one in the one Spirit.)

John 14:16–17 (The Spirit is with us always.)

Acts 1:1–5 (Jesus taught through the Holy Spirit and promised baptism with the Holy Spirit.)

Acts 2:1–13 (The Holy Spirit comes at Pentecost.)

Acts 10:4–48 (The Holy Spirit comes to Gentiles.)

Acts 19:1–7 (Believers in Jesus receive the Holy Spirit.)

Every believer in this world must become a spark of light.

Pope John XXIII

Resolutions for Sponsors

To help the candidate I am sponsoring celebrate the sacrament of confirmation and live the deeper faith and the more active life in Christ's Church that it signifies, I resolve the following:

1. _____

2. _____

3. _____

4. _____

5. _____

Prayers for Confirmation

Come, Holy Spirit

Come, Holy Spirit, fill the hearts of your faithful,
and kindle in them the fire of your love.
Send forth your spirit and they shall be created,
and you shall renew the face of the earth.

O God, who does instruct the hearts of the faithful
by the light of the Holy Spirit,
grant us by that same Holy Spirit,
to relish what is right and just,
and always rejoice in your consolation.
We ask this through Jesus Christ, our Lord.
Amen.

Prayer of St. Augustine

Breathe in me, O Holy Spirit, that my thoughts be holy. Act in me, O Holy Spirit, that all I do may be holy. Draw me on and open wide my heart to your love. Strengthen me, O Holy Spirit, to defend all that is holy. Guard me then, O Holy Spirit. Guide me now that I may be holy, always wholly yours.

Prayer of Cardinal Newman

Lord, Jesus, help me to spread your fragrance everywhere. Flood me with your spirit and life; penetrate and possess my whole being so completely that my life may be only a radiance of yours. Shine through me and be so in me that everyone with whom I come into contact may feel your presence within me. Let them look up and no longer see me, but only you, Jesus.

Learning Christ

Teach me, my Lord, to be sweet and gentle in all the events of my life: in disappointments, in the thoughtlessness of others, in the insincerity of those I trusted, in the unfaithfulness of those on whom I relied.

Let me put myself aside to think of the happiness of others, to hide my little pains and heartaches so that I may be the only one to suffer from them. Teach me to profit by the suffering that comes across my path. Let me so use it that it may mellow me, nor harden or embitter me; that it may make me patient, not irritable; that it may make me broad in my forgiveness, not narrow, haughty, or overbearing.

May no one be less good for having come within my influence. No one less pure, less true, less kind, less noble for having been a fellow traveler in our journey toward eternal life.

As I go my rounds from one distraction to another, let me whisper from time to time a word of love to you. May my life be lived in the supernatural, full of power for good, and strong in its purpose of sanctity.

Prayer of St. Benedict

O gracious and holy Father,
give us wisdom to perceive
    you,
intelligence to understand
    you,
diligence to seek you,
patience to wait for you,
eyes to see you,
a heart to meditate on you,
and a life to proclaim you,
through the power
of the Spirit of Jesus Christ
    our Lord.

Prayer to the Holy Spirit

Come, Holy Spirit, fill my heart with your holy gifts. Let my weakness be penetrated with your strength this very day that I may fulfill all the duties of my state conscientiously, that I may do what is right and just.

Let my charity be such as to offend no one, and hurt no one's feelings; so generous as to pardon sincerely any wrong done to me.

Assist me, O Holy Spirit, in my trials of life, enlighten me in my ignorance, advise me in my doubts, strengthen me in my weakness, help me in all my needs, protect me in temptations and console me in afflictions.

Graciously hear me, O Holy Spirit, and pour your light into my heart, my soul, and my mind.

Assist me to live a holy life and to grow in goodness and grace.

Amen.

You are not only free, but also holy; not only holy, but also just; not only just, but also daughters and sons; not only daughters and sons, but also heirs; not only heirs, but brothers and sisters; not only brothers and sisters, but also joint heirs; not only joint heirs, but also members; not only members, but also the temple; not only the temple, but also the instruments of the Spirit!

St. John Chrysostom

Other Resources for Confirmation Sponsors

INVITATION TO CATHOLICISM
Alice Camille
Everyone from inquirers and catechumens to lifelong Catholics will welcome the easy-to-understand, logical explanations found in this clear, concise overview of Catholic beliefs and Church teachings. God, Jesus, Mary and the saints, the Bible, Mass, sacraments and prayer, plus moral and virtuous Christian living are all presented in a gentle yet persuasive manner. (240 pages, $9.95)

PRAYER: A PRACTICAL GUIDE
Rev. Martin Pable, OFM Cap.
An introduction to the Catholic approach to prayer, including traditional prayer, conversational prayer, prayer with Scripture, group prayer and the Mass as prayer. Includes questions for reflection and prayer activities. (96 pages, $9.95)

LIFE IN CHRIST: A CATHOLIC CATECHISM FOR ADULTS
Revs. Gerard Weber and James Kilgallon
Written in the traditional question-and-answer format, this is the #1 adult Catholic catechism. Extensively revised in accordance with the *Catechism of the Catholic Church*, it contains hundreds of scriptural references and quotations. (336 pages, $6.95)

THE MASS: AN INVITATION TO ENJOY IT
Amy Florian
A warm and gentle explanation of the Catholic Mass, presented in easy-to-understand language filled with helpful examples. (96 pages, $9.95)

Available from booksellers or call 800-397-2282 in the U.S. or Canada.

Other Books in This Series

THE GIFT OF BAPTISM
TOM SHERIDAN
A welcoming book that teaches parents about the meaning of the sacrament and helps them understand their role as parents. 64 pages, paperback, $4.95

THE GIFT OF GODPARENTS
TOM SHERIDAN
Information about the sacrament of baptism and the responsibilities of godparenting are blended with touching stories and suggestions. 96 pages, paperback, $5.95

THE GIFT OF CONFIRMATION
SISTER KATHLEEN GLAVICH
Explanation and suggestions for parents of children being confirmed, including much of the information contained in *The Gift of Confirmation Sponsors.* 80 pages, paperback, $4.95

THE GIFT OF HOLY COMMUNION
SISTER KATHLEEN GLAVICH
A book that explains the Eucharist to parents of children receiving Communion for the first time and gives them the words to use when talking with their children about the sacrament. 80 pages, paperback, $4.95

THE GIFT OF RECONCILIATION
SISTER KATHLEEN GLAVICH
Presents to parents the meaning and importance of confession, penance and reconciliation for their children—and themselves. 80 pages, paperback, $4.95

Available from booksellers or call 800-397-2282